PIANO/VOCAL/GUITAR

JUSTIN TIMBERLAKE
FUTURESEX/LOVESOUNDS

Published by
Wise Publications
14-15 Berners Street, London W1T 3LJ, UK.

Exclusive Distributors:
Music Sales Limited
Distribution Centre, Newmarket Road, Bury St. Edmunds, Suffolk IP33 3YB, UK.
Music Sales Pty Limited
120 Rothschild Avenue, Rosebury, NSW 2018, Australia.

Order No. AM990077
ISBN 13: 978-1-84772-031-3
This book © Copyright 2007 Wise Publications.

Printed in the USA.

www.musicsales.com

Wise Publications
part of The Music Sales Group
London/New York/Paris/Sydney/Copenhagen/Berlin/Madrid/Tokyo

FUTURESEX/LOVESOUND

Words and Music by JUSTIN TIMBERLAKE,
TIM MOSLEY and NATE HILLS

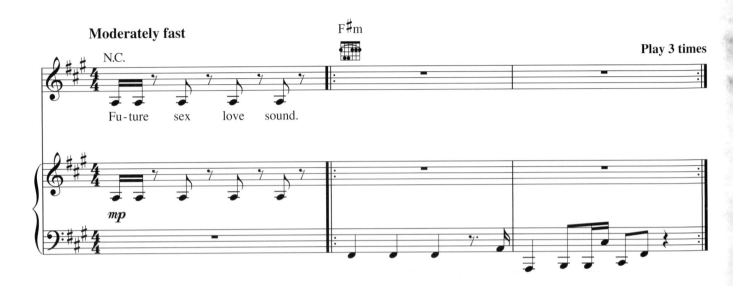

See, ev-'ry-bod-y says you're hot, ba - by,

but can you make it hot for me?

Said, if you're think-ing 'bout hold - ing back, don't wor - ry, girl, ____

'cause I'm gon-na make it so eas - y.

Tell me which way you like ___ that.

Uh - huh, ___ huh, huh, oh.

Tell me which way you like ___ that.

Fu - ture sex love sound.

Fu - ture sex love sound.

SEXYBACK

Words and Music by JUSTIN TIMBERLAKE,
TIM MOSLEY and NATE HILLS

Ooh,   ooh,   ooh,   ahh, __ ooh.

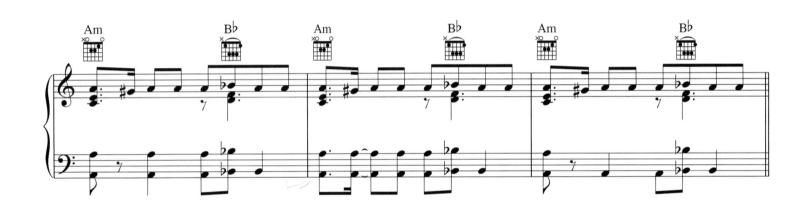

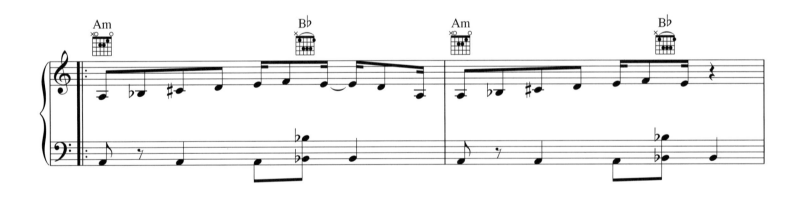

Repeat and Fade | **Optional Ending**

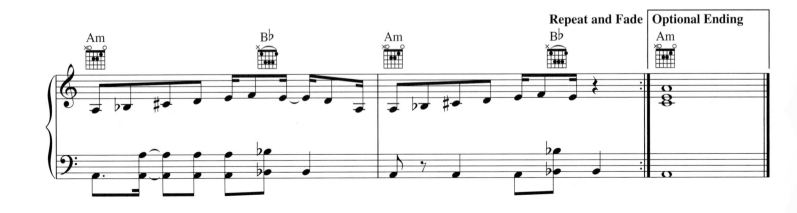

SEXY LADIES
Let Me Talk to You (Prelude)

Words and Music by JUSTIN TIMBERLAKE,
TIM MOSLEY and NATE HILLS

I can tell you want a drink, girl, you ain't got-ta wor-ry no more.__
girl-y from up - town who's wait-in' just to ca-ter to me.__

They keep my bot-tles cold and they pop 'em as soon as I walk in the door.__
I know a lit-tle Bet-ty from down-town that'll do an-y-thing that I please.__

These dudes __ don't know me from Ad-am and Eve, that's why they can't mess up my flow.__
All, __ my p - peo-ple, they dance __ 'round __ when they hear me rock-in' the groove.__

Recorded a half step lower.

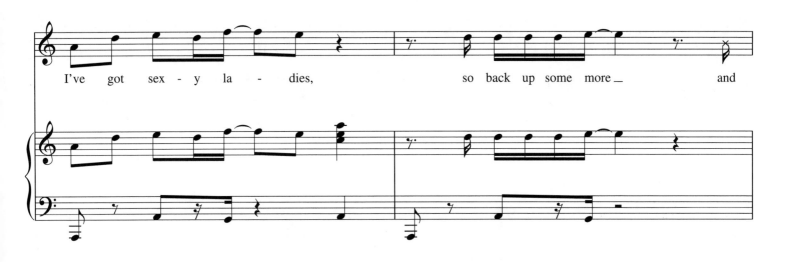

I've got sex - y la - dies, so back up some more __ and

let me take it off.

Play 3 times

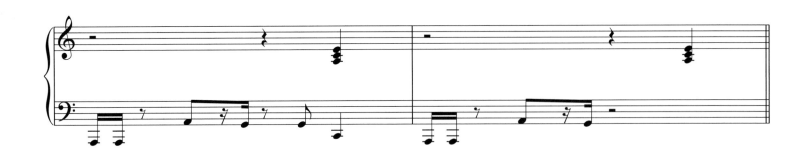

Play 3 times

Moderately fast

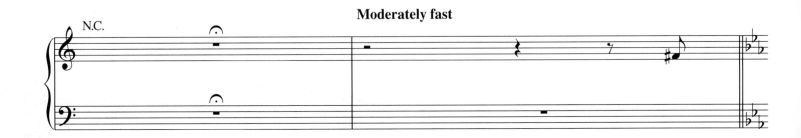

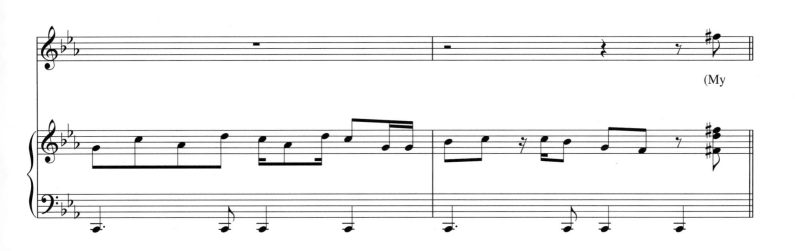

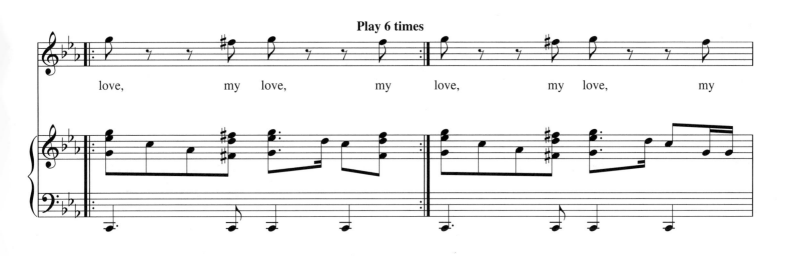

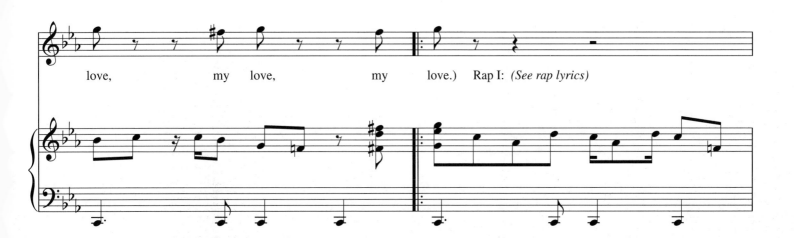

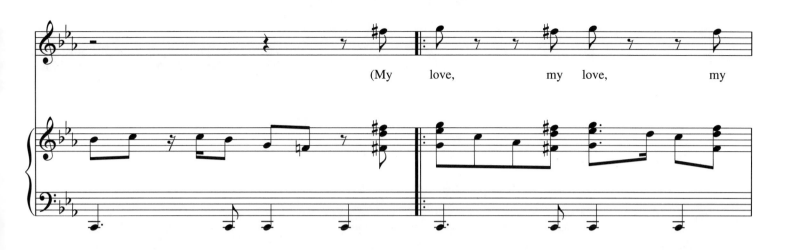

(My love, my love, my

Play 3 times

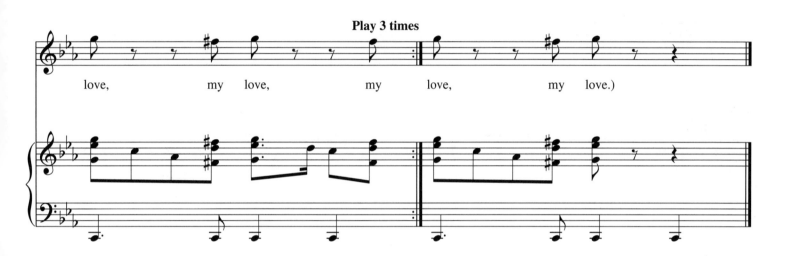

love, my love, my love, my love.)

Rap Lyrics

Rap I: I love the way you standin'.
Lips look so sweet, like cotton candy.
That don't mean you gotta stop dancin',
'Cause the way that you move is so demandin'.
Let's put it on cruise control.
Let me take you to the crib, let me ease your soul.
I'm gonna take it nice and slow,
But first, let me, let me, let me talk to her.

Rap II: Walk into my great place, cozy,
I'm glad you came. Let's make a toast to...
Let me make an indecent proposal,
Let me take you to the back and do what we supposed to.
Let's take a trip to Dubai.
You can be the investigator, I'm your private eye.
You know I want a piece of that pie,
But first, let me, let me, let me talk to her.

MY LOVE

Words and Music by JUSTIN TIMBERLAKE,
TIM MOSLEY, NATE HILLS and CLIFFORD HARRIS

Ain't an - oth - er wom-an that could take your spot my...

I can see us hold-ing hands,

Additional Lyrics

Rap: Alright, it's time to get it J.T. I don't know what she hesitating for, man.
    Hey – Shorty cool as a fan and I knew once again and he still has fans from Peru to Japan.
    Hey, listen baby, I don't wanna ruin your plan (naw) but if you got a man, try to lose him if you can.
    'Cause the girl's real wild, throw your hands up high when you wanna come and kick it with a stand-up guy.
    Trust me, you don't really wanna let the chance go by 'cause you ain't been seen with a man so fly.
    Hey baby, friends so fly. I can go fly private 'cause I handle my B-I.
    They call me candle guy. (Why?) Simply 'cause I am on fire. I hate to have to cancel my vacation.
    So you can't deny I'm patient but I ain't gonna try, naw. You don't come, I ain't gonna die.
    Hold up, what you mean you can't go – why? Me and your boyfriend, we ain't no tie.
    You say you wanna kick it when I ain't so high. Well, baby, it's obvious that I ain't your guy.
    I ain't gonna lie, I feel your space, but forget your face. I swear I will.
    St. Barts, Anguilla, anywhere I chill. Just bring with me a pair I will.

LOVESTONED
I Think She Knows (Interlude)

Words and Music by JUSTIN TIMBERLAKE,
TIM MOSLEY and NATE HILLS

Those flash - in' lights come from ev - 'ry - where.

The way they hit her, I just stop and stare.

She's got me love - stoned.

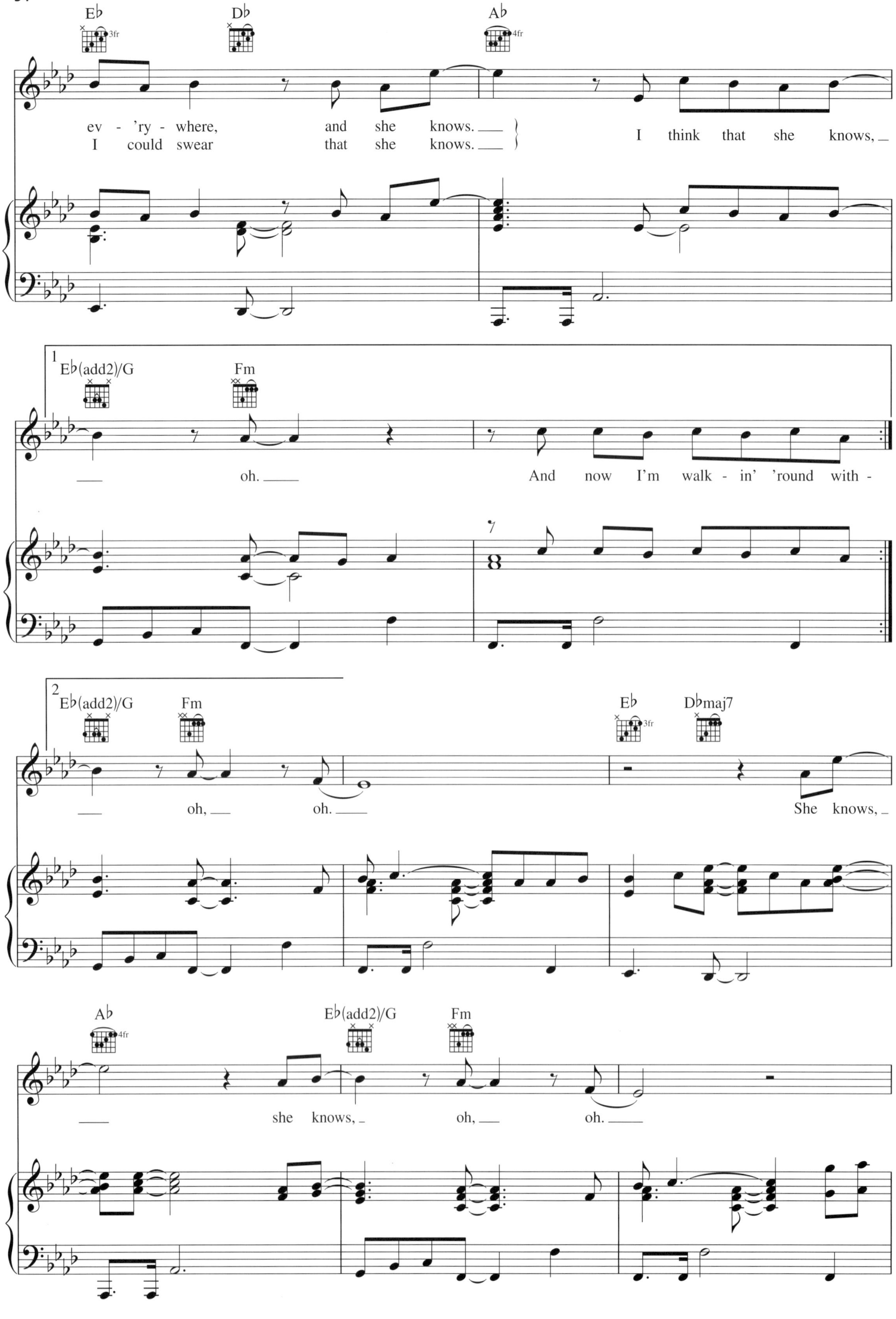

E♭
D♭
A♭
3fr
4fr
ev - 'ry - where, and she knows.
I could swear that she knows.
I think that she knows,
1
E♭(add2)/G
Fm
oh.
And now I'm walk - in' 'round with -
2
E♭(add2)/G
Fm
E♭
D♭maj7
oh, oh.
She knows,
A♭
E♭(add2)/G
Fm
she knows, oh, oh.

WHAT GOES AROUND
...Comes Around (Interlude)

Words and Music by JUSTIN TIMBERLAKE,
TIM MOSLEY and NATE HILLS

CHOP ME UP

Words and Music by JUSTIN TIMBERLAKE,
TIM MOSLEY and NATE HILLS

Recorded a half step lower.

Lit - tle la - dy (la - dy, la - dy), you got me just

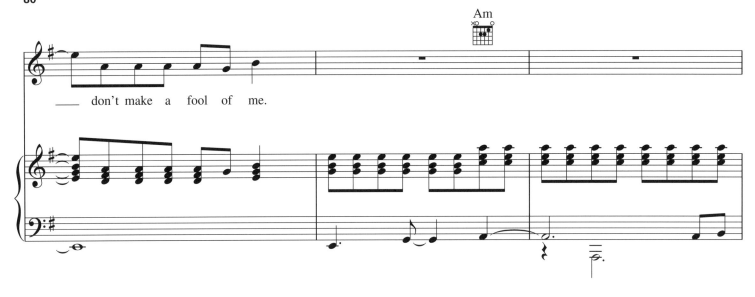

don't make a fool of me.

Rap Lyrics

See, girl, you stronger than the strongest drug I ever had.
You could mix them all together; you'd still be twice as bad,
'Cause you're the worst best girlfriend I ever had.
Harder to kick than cigarettes and green bags,
Harder to escape than jail cells and bills mailed.
You had me locked since a bitty girl with pigtails.
Like Michael Jackson, (Why you do me this way?)
Got me cryin' rivers like Timbaland and Timberlake, yeah.
They call me Juicy J, straight up out the Three-6 Mafia.
Ghetto fab player, all these freaks and I'm tryin' to holla at ya.
Quit playin' games, girl, you got my head spinnin' 'round.
I ain't gonna chirp your mobile phone and chase you all over town.
I just want to pick you up and take you to a wrestling match then
(So is it good, is it good) and have a little smack fest.
So if you never call me, I'll be somewhere down in Tennessee,
Washin' away my sorrows in a cold cup of Hennessy.

DAMN GIRL

Words and Music by JUSTIN TIMBERLAKE,
WILL ADAMS, JOSH DAVIS and J.C. DAVIS

Moderately fast

Damn, _ girl, damn, _ girl, damn, _ girl, damn, _ girl, damn, _ girl, damn. _

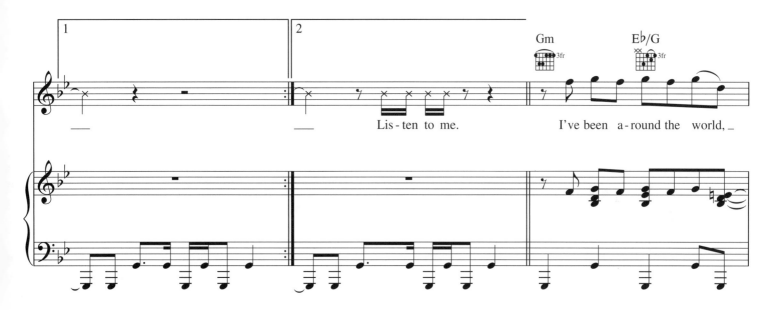

Lis-ten to me. I've been a-round the world, _

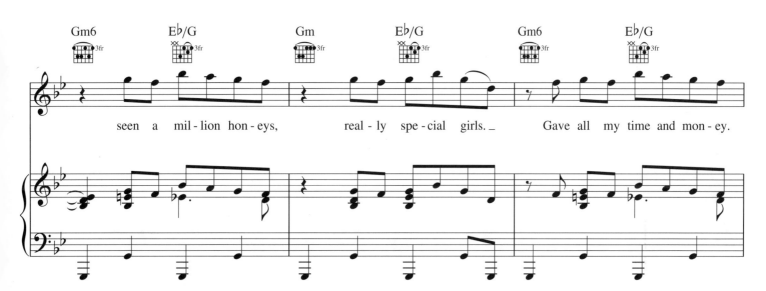

seen a mil-lion hon-eys, real-ly spe-cial girls. _ Gave all my time and mon-ey.

Damn, — girl, damn, — girl, damn, — girl, damn, —

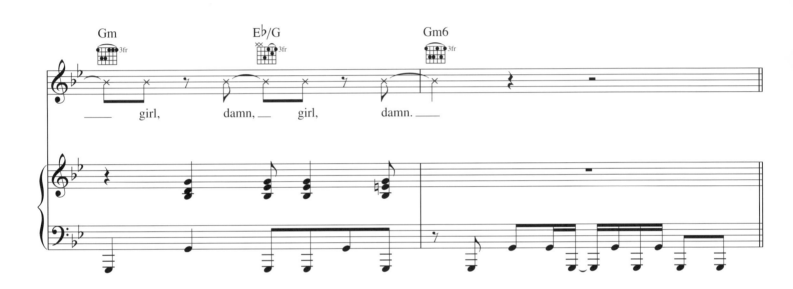

— girl, damn, — girl, damn. —

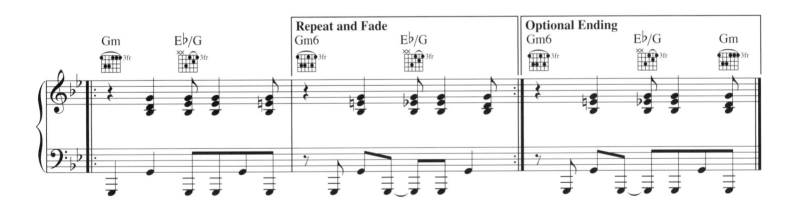

Rap Lyrics

Woo, woo, woo, woo, woo, woo, woo, woo, woo, woo baby.
Give me some of your tasty cinnamon.
Givin' your feminine gelatin,
'Cause got a cinnamon goin' crazy.
Hey, b-b-b-b-b-b-baby,
Baby, you're the one I been feindin' for.
When I'm dreamin', I'm dreamin' of you.
When you're gone, I'll be screamin' for you.

So why don't you be my chick and stuff?
Take you out to dinner and catch a flick and stuff.
If we spend time I never get enough.
Girl, you're so fine, make a dark brother blush.
Got me lookin' like a black grape and stuff.
First time I seen you, you had me on crush.
And if you ever give it to me, give it to me rough.
You got me sayin', got me sayin', "Damn."

SUMMER LOVE
Set the Mood (Prelude)

Words and Music by JUSTIN TIMBERLAKE,
TIM MOSLEY and NATE HILLS

(L - O - V - E.)
love.

(Spoken:) Yeah.

Slowly, steadily

Come here, baby.

UNTIL THE END OF TIME

Words and Music by JUSTIN TIMBERLAKE,
TIM MOSLEY and NATE HILLS

I woke up this morn - ing and heard the
Now if you're ev - er won - d'ring a -

T - V say - ing some - thing a - bout di - sas - ter in the world, and
bout the way I'm feel - ing, well, ba - by girl, there ain't no ques - tion.

yeah, — yeah, — yeah. — (Yeah, — yeah, — yeah.) —

yeah, — — yeah. — (Yeah, — — yeah.) —

This one's for the lov - ers. If you're out there, let me hear you say,

yeah, — yeah, yeah, — yeah. (Yeah, — yeah, yeah, — yeah.)

LOSING MY WAY

Words and Music by JUSTIN TIMBERLAKE,
TIM MOSLEY and NATE HILLS

Lyrics:

Hi, my name is Bob __ and I work at my job. __ I make for-ty-some-thin' dol-lars a day. __

got-ta un-der-stand, I was a fam-'ly man, __ I would have done __ an-y-thing for my own. __ But I

Recorded a half step lower.

(Another Song)
ALL OVER AGAIN

Words and Music by JUSTIN TIMBERLAKE
and MATTHEW B. MORRIS

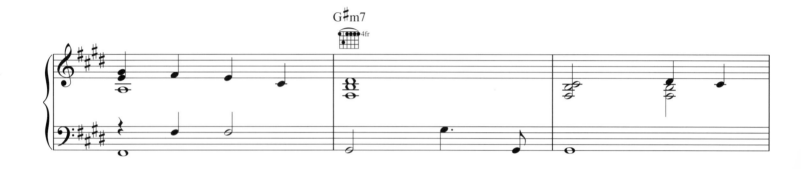

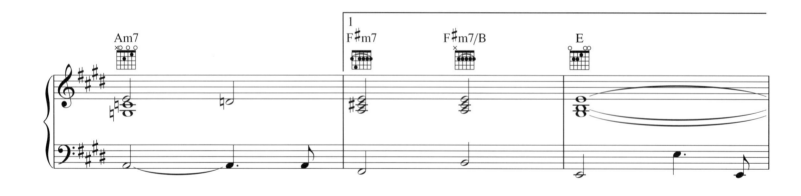

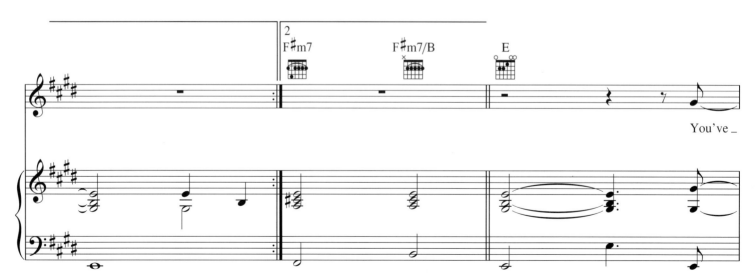

You've _

Gm7
F♯m7
F♯m7/B
might try and love me. So
E
E/G♯
please give me an - oth - er chance
A
to write you an - oth - er song and take back
Am6
B
A
G♯m7
those things I've done, 'cause I'll give you